Going Higher

A Coffee & Scriptures Devotional:
Revised Edition

12 Weeks of Reflection for the Woman of God

Tara Tucker

A Coffee & Scriptures Devotional

To:_____

From:_____

Date: _____

Note:_____
_____
_____
_____
_____
_____
_____

Going Higher

Going Higher

12 weeks of Reflection for the Woman of God

Revised Edition

TARA TUCKER

Copyright © 2018-2021 Tara Tucker

Published Revised Edition | Warren, Michigan | USA

8/2021 Tucker Publishing House, LLC.

All rights reserved. No part of this book may be reproduced in any form without permission, in writing, from the publisher, except in the case of brief quotations in articles or reviews. All websites listed herein are accurate at the time of publication but may change in the future or cease to exist. The publisher is not endorsing any website, group, or corporation. If any are listed, it does not imply an endorsement.

Scriptures, unless otherwise noted, were taken from the King James Version (KJV.)

The Message. Copyright © 1993, 1994, 1995, 1996, 2000, 2001, 2002. Used by permission of NavPress Publishing Group."

Scripture quotations marked (NLT) are taken from the Holy Bible, New Living Translation, Copyright © 1996, 2004, 2007, 2013, 2015 by Tyndale House Foundation. Used by permission of Tyndale House Publishers, Inc., Carol Stream, Illinois 60188. All rights reserved

Paperback ISBN: 978-1-7344526-9-3

www.tuckerpublishinghouse.com

OTHER BOOKS BY TARA TUCKER

Screams from the Church Pew "Her Story, God's Glory" Anthology

Everybody Kneeling ain't Praying – A Memoir

You Are Not Disqualified (How to let go of your past and move forward in purpose)

Coffee & Scriptures Devotionals

Going Higher (1st Edition)

An Amazing Discovery

Trusting God During the Journey

DEDICATION

"This book is dedicated to all the women of God who are fighting this good fight of faith. Remember, the human experience is a shared one. We're in this together!"

~ Tara Tucker

TABLE OF CONTENTS

Dedication **vii**

Table of Contents **viii**

Introduction **1**

Week 1 Grace **7**

Week 2 Obedience **12**

Week 3 Endurance **16**

Week 4 Discipline **21**

SUMMARY OF WEEKS 1-4 **26**

Week 5 Identity **27**

Week 6 Faith **32**

Week 7 Prayer **37**

Week 8 Fasting **42**

SUMMARY OF WEEKS 5-8 **47**

Week 9 Double-mindedness **48**

Week 10: Renewal **53**

- Week 11 SIN. **58**
- Week 12 Freedom **63**
- SUMMARY OF WEEKS 9–12 **67**
- Word-based Affirmations **68**
- References **69**
- Afterward **70**
- Acknowledgements **71**
- ABOUT THE AUTHOR **73**

INTRODUCTION

In October of 2016, with the leading of the Lord, I started a prayer group, JEWELS, Ladies of Prayer. (now Jewels LOP Outreach) We pray and study together weekly. We meet up every three months to have our "Sister Talk" meetings, removing the metaphorical mask we often wear as women. Also, each day we send scriptures and Words of encouragement. I thought to extend that encouragement to my other sisters in Christ. That would be *you*.

> You must warn each other every day, while it is still "today," so that none of you will be deceived by sin and hardened against God.
>
> **Hebrews 3:13 NLT.**

I'm a woman of God who's had heavy trials before *and* after being saved by God's Grace. A woman who's decided to trust and seriously follow Jesus. A woman who has lived a lifestyle quite contrary to the one she lives now and thankful for God's saving grace. I've had many trials and tribulations in this world, as Jesus said that we would. I have wisdom and knowledge that I've gained from the streets and the Lord. God has increased my spiritual discernment, and I *see* clearer than I ever have.

Focal Point

I focus on women in my writings because, as a woman, I understand the daily struggles of a career woman, single woman, stay-at-home wife, and mother, etc. I have been all of those. I am also a fellow believer. We must be strong in our faith and walk this thing out together! I know that it can feel like you're spinning your wheels, with good intentions yet bad outcomes - feeling overworked and under-appreciated. Can you relate? I feel this way as well many times, but God appreciates me. He appreciates us. And if we do things with the Lord in mind, He will be our reward. We cannot get tired in well-doing.

We are a worldwide spiritual family. We all need to focus on growth in the Lord and spiritual matters, especially as the day of the Lord approaches. The Lord showed me that we must get *our* houses in order before we can help others. That's our spiritual and natural houses. Who's listening to us if we aren't practicing what we preach? Let's be real. And we should be first showing changed behavior as Christian women in our households which will then extend outwards.

We carry a lot on our shoulders, and it can get heavy. As believers in God, we are stronger together, and must encourage each other.

"Going Higher" was written particularly for the woman of God – the believing woman who may not be exactly where she wants to be in her walk with God. She may be struggling with finding just who she is in God and what He expects of her. She may desire a deeper relationship and more revelations but is unaware of how to attain it.

My Story

I've walked this walk for the past ten years. Before that, I was a Jehovah's Witness. The Lord came into my life like a whirlwind and changed it completely. Even after, it took years to renew my mind to where it is now. It's a gradual process. The Lord "saved" me even *after* I was saved.

I was diagnosed with stage 3 breast cancer in December of 2016. Through my trial of fighting cancer, the Lord revealed Himself to me in miraculous ways. He sat me down from work, church, and more. I was in the wilderness, and it was one of the loneliest experiences of my life.

He shifted my entire life and instructed me to write about it to help others. That will happen through a series of books in the order that He has determined. The teachings in this book will show you how you can have the relationship you seek with God. You'll abide in His perfect peace despite any situation. You'll learn what it means to be truly free and never succumb to bondage again.

God is real. He is alive, and He loves us. When He says that ALL things work together for our good, believe Him. Don't be discouraged a moment longer. Be encouraged and fight the good fight of faith! I am your sister in Christ, and I am fighting alongside you.

My advice is to begin your day with prayer, your favorite beverage, the Bible, and this great devotional! Choose a time with little to no distractions. You can also choose to do it in the evenings. You must do whichever is best to give you the most benefits. During self-reflection, you must ponder what is being asked of you.

What you will find in the subsequent pages is a quote from me, a scripture, reflections, challenge questions, prayers, and end-of-month summaries.

For the next 12 weeks, read these devotionals and scriptures and reflect on the questions. Be honest with where you are. Challenge yourself to go where you want to be. Set a time each day and stick to it. Commit to yourself. If it's 7:00 am or noon, whatever, make an appointment with God and keep it. He also honors it, and it keeps you accountable.

You can also use it in group study. Grab a few of your girls and go through the devotionals together.

Read, pray, and reflect. I repeat, read, pray, and reflect. (Not necessarily in that order.) You will start to see a difference in your committed walk with God.

First and foremost, understand that you must be *intentional* in your worship if you want to go higher. Furthermore, you must not go through your walk just reacting to everything that happens to you. You must make some intentional moves – doing things "on purpose." You will read that Word a lot *(intentional)* because it's paramount in elevating.

We learn through repetition. I read somewhere that repetition leads to belief, which in turn becomes a deep conviction. If you do the same thing for a certain time, it will get ingrained in you. By studying, and reflecting on one topic for the week, I hope you truly learn and believe what the Word says about you. Write in this devotional. Use the margins and a notebook; it's personal. Once it's complete, put it to the side. One day in the coming months or years, check back and see where you were.

Your responses are between you and God. Be honest when you answer the reflection questions.

PRAY

Father God, I come to you today through Jesus' name, asking for strength to get through the coming weeks. Lord, I want to be consistent in my worship for you. I want to come to you openly and honestly. Turn your face to me, Lord. I come humbly before you, knowing that I can do nothing apart from you. Father, open my ears to hear and my eyes to see what your Spirit is saying. I thank you for your reminders, your Word, and your people. I ask that you create a clean heart and renew a right spirit within me because I want to serve you wholeheartedly. Father, forgive me in any areas where I have disappointed you in thought or deed. Keep the tempter from me, Jesus, and grant me a willing spirit. Keep me protected and cover me under the shadow of your wings. Lord, I love you and thank you for striving with me. I thank you for not giving up on me. I promise to give you honor, glory, and praise. In Jesus name, Amen

WEEKLY DEVOTIONALS

WEEK 1: GRACE

Grace is free, but leveling up is not

WEEKLY REFLECTIONS

Charis, the Greek word for grace, is defined as unmerited favor, blessing, or kindness. Unmerited means that we didn't do anything to earn it. God loves us so much that He bestows grace on us. A gift! He gives us favor. He chooses to bless us rather than punish us as our sin deserves. We know we fall short, and sometimes we feel that we are not enough or aren't doing enough. We may feel like we can't measure up to what God wants.

> Each time he said, "My grace is all you need. My power works best in weakness." So now I am glad to boast about my weaknesses so that the power of Christ can work through me.
>
> **2 Corinthians 12:9 NLT**

That's the human part of us, and it's ok. But it's important to note that God does not condemn us - He corrects us. The enemy condemns us. He tells us that we can't make it. He tells us that we are a failure and can't stop a bad habit. He says to us that we are unable to conquer it, and it's too hard. So just give in to it. You only live once, right? So, do whatever you want! That's how the enemy works. The battleground is our mind. Let's not entertain those thoughts. (2 Corinthians 10:5)

It's important to start the right relationship with God. Start with the understanding that you fall short, but there is an intercessor for you, our Lord Jesus Christ.

God says His grace is sufficient for us. Sufficiency means it's enough for us—He is enough for us. And we are enough for Him because He meets us where we are. We don't have to beat ourselves up or figure out everything.

Jesus fills in the gaps! Brag on His strengths! Brag on, Jesus! Let Him show Himself in your life by understanding your weaknesses and allow Him to show His strength.

He loves you with an everlasting love! And sometimes it's hard to receive because you aren't used to it. You are used to how things have always been. But slowly, as you continue day by day to trust Him, you'll find each day becomes easier. Tomorrow will have its own worries. (Matthew 6:34)

It's less overwhelming when you do it this way. We're bombarded with distractions, stressors, etc., and it's necessary to be aware but not consumed. Gods got you. He's got me—we, who profess Him and follow Him. Yes, God has *us*. Rest in that truth today. Resting in God's grace gives you peace that you wouldn't normally have. It allows you to respond in kindness when people are unkind. It will enable you to treat people how they don't deserve, just as He does with us. Resting in His grace changes you. You'll start to walk in it, but you must recognize that it's there and available for you. As you grow in your knowledge of Him, you grow in your love. As your love and understanding deepen, your desires change. You *want* to live right and do the right thing *because* you love Him.

I used to beat myself up when I failed. I had a smoking habit. I remember wanting to stop smoking and feeling bad that I couldn't. What I didn't understand is that I wasn't yielding to God. He had grace for me. I had to accept my limitations—admit that I could only go so far. I needed Him. I had to depend on Him daily. I was weak, but where I was weak, He was strong! He proved Himself strong in my life.

I started to understand that God loved me despite my mess. I was enough, and He would meet me where I was. That helped me tremendously. Just to come to that realization that God loves me even though my shortcomings did wonders for me. To learn that I wasn't too "messed up" for Him helped me lean in closer. The fact was, I didn't have to clean myself up before approaching Him; He would do that.

God is your Father, and He wants the very best for you. Grace is amazing, and you should live a life of gratitude because of how wonderful our Heavenly Father has been. He treats us better than we deserve. Let's be intentional in our walk with Him. Let's walk honest and upright, knowing that we did nothing to deserve the blessings. It's just because He is good.

PRAY

Lord God of Grace, thank you for waking me this morning. Lord, I pray that you go before me and set my path straight. It is not up to me to direct my steps. I look to you, Lord, who is the author and finisher of my faith. Help me align my thoughts with yours, Lord. Search me and show me what I need to work on. I am praying for clarity and focus. Lord, today I surrender my problems to you. I surrender my children, my job, my health, my marriage, my vehicles, my mind, my emotions, my life, and my way! I surrender it all to you, Lord. I want your will to be done in my life Lord. I say yes to your will and yes to your way! Where I am weak, you are strong. Show yourself to me today, Lord. Show your strength in my life in the name of Jesus. You say in your Word that you will teach me the ways of wisdom and lead me in straight paths. I'm standing on your Word and believing you. You lead, and I will follow, trusting that you will never leave me or forsake me. Thank you, Lord. In Jesus name, Amen

YOUR WEEKLY CHALLENGE

This week ask yourself these reflection questions and look up the scriptures that are listed below. Read, pray, and meditate on what it says about grace. Write down your answers.

John 1:14-17 | Romans 11:6 | James 4:6 | Hebrews 4:16 | John 1:17 | Ephesians 2:4-9 | 1 Corinthians 15:10

What is God's grace exactly? How has God's grace shown up in my life?

How does grace make me see myself? And God?

Do I show grace to others? In what ways? Do I show it when they've angered me?

Do I worry about the future? Why or why not? How do I handle conflict?

Do I highlight my weaknesses? Or other weaknesses? Am I arrogant or humble? Would others agree?

How do I show my appreciation for the Lord? Do I sometimes take Him for granted?

Do I thank God daily regardless of my situation? Or do I complain? Do I lean on Him every day? Or myself?

WEEK 2: OBEDIENCE

You won't elevate in disobedience

Weekly Reflections

Obedience is one of the principal factors in following the Lord. When you live a life of obedience, you are walking in confidence. You know that you are doing what the Lord says of you to do, so you go boldly to the throne. When you aren't, you feel unsure of yourself. You are not sure if the Lord hears your prayer.

Obedience is the act or practice of obeying. It's something we do, and not just say. It's compliance. We must reverence our God and give Him the respect that is due Him by obeying. The Word of God was written for our benefit. It corrects us and teaches us how to live right. (2 Timothy 3:16)

Let's obey it and not say "No" to God. You may ask yourself, "When did I say, No?" You say it when the Word He gave you is not followed by you. You're saying "No" when *your* will goes before His. You're saying "No" when what He told you is too uncomfortable or painful for you to do, so you don't do it even though you can actually learn obedience through your suffering.

Your mouth may say "Yes," but your actions speak something else. God wants obedience. He says that it's better than sacrifice, and we know sacrifice is important. He isn't fooled by what we say.

We are the same way with our children. We want them to listen to us; We love them and know best. We are wiser and have experienced more in life. God is our Father and deals with us similarly, as a Father to a daughter. I'm thankful for His love and mercy towards us. He is long-suffering towards us.

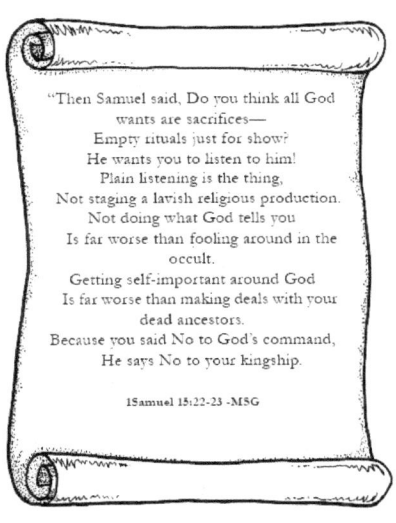

"Then Samuel said, Do you think all God wants are sacrifices—
Empty rituals just for show?
He wants you to listen to him!
Plain listening is the thing,
Not staging a lavish religious production.
Not doing what God tells you
Is far worse than fooling around in the occult.
Getting self-important around God
Is far worse than making deals with your dead ancestors.
Because you said No to God's command,
He says No to your kingship.

1Samuel 15:22-23 -MSG

God gives us instructions from the pulpit, through His Word, people, in prayer, and dreams, just to name a few. We read the Word, and it is alive as it says in Hebrews 4:12. The Word shows us how we ought to live. God uses the fivefold ministry: Teachers, Pastors, Evangelist, Apostles, Prophets for the body of believers. He can use anyone He wants to get a Word to you, and He will. The question is, "What will you do once you hear His voice?" (Hebrews 3:15)

When you pray and sit quietly in His presence, He will reveal things to you. It doesn't always happen right away. You must press into it. Be intentional about it. Many times, we give up because we don't hear Him right away. However, the more you subject yourself to Him, the more you will listen with your spiritual ears. He also comes in dreams. I have them often. (Job 33:15)

The Lord is speaking. We just have to quiet all the outside noise to hear Him. And you must be in your Word so that you know how

His voice sounds. You don't want to get confused by listening to the enemy or yourself.

Obedience is required to go higher in God. Start obeying today.

PRAY

Lord, I thank you for another day. I ask for your forgiveness Lord for things I've done in thought or deed that you have disapproved of. I thank you for your grace, love, and mercy. Go before me this day, Lord, and set my path straight. I can do nothing apart from you, God, so I am asking for direction. Help me to walk by faith and not sight. Create in me a clean heart and renew a right spirit within me, Lord. Keep me on the Potters' wheel—Less of me and more of you. Help me in my disobedience Lord. I want to obey! Help me, Jesus! I know that it is out of love that we walk in obedience to your commands. I do love you, Lord. Increase my faith, Lord. I want to say yes to your will and your way and walk in your truths. In Jesus name, Amen

YOUR WEEKLY CHALLENGE

This week ask yourself these reflection questions and look up the scriptures that are listed below. Read, pray, and meditate on what it says about obedience. Write down your answers.

James 1:22 | 2 Corinthians 10:5 | Romans 6:16 | John 14: 23-24 | Luke 9:23-25 | 1 Samuel 15: 1-23 | Proverbs 4:10-15

What does the Word say about obedience? How important is obedience in my growth with God?

Have I been obedient? What type of attitude do I have?

What can I do to show my obedience daily? At home? At work? At church?

Why is obedience better than sacrifice?

How do I react when God chastises me? Do I accept correction? Why or Why not?

Do I respect and obey my leaders in the faith? Do I regularly attend church? Why or why not? Do I follow the laws of the land? Or do I choose which ones to follow? Do I walk the line?

Do I know God's voice? How? What voices have I been listening to? Who else speaks to me? How do I respond to all these different voices?

WEEK 3: ENDURANCE

Go through and GROW through

WEEKLY REFLECTIONS

Things or circumstances are not removed or changed right away because God knows what He is doing. We must wait. He may be trying to show you who you are, who He is, work something out of you, or even in you. He may be preparing you for a place or preparing a place for you.

> In everything we do, we show that we are true ministers of God. We patiently endure troubles and hardships and calamities of every kind.
>
> 2 Corinthians 6:4 NLT

These are just a few examples. He works our patience and endurance thru our waiting. God's thoughts and ways are not ours, and they are so much better and higher. He allows us to make decisions. *We* sometimes make the wrong decisions, and *we* suffer the consequences of our actions. It is not always the devil or God.

Thankfully, He has mercy on us. You may think something should change in your situation immediately and want to give up. We can't give up when it hurts and when it's hard. You will get nowhere giving up. I promise you. Your faith will get nowhere giving up. Wait. I stand corrected; your faith will decrease. I don't want that to happen. It's a downward spiral with a domino effect.

Push through. Go through and *grow* through! Wait during your trials with joy, peace, and the expectation that all will be well according to God's will. To do that, you must trust Him. Trust that He will see you through.

Yes, you will go through, but the refining that comes upon you is undeniable. The spiritual maturation is amazing, and the sense of self is refreshing. Your eyes will be opened, and you will realize how blind you were. Allow God to work a good thing in you. Submit to His love and authority.

Many want the blessings and benefits that come as a child of God walking in obedience, but they don't want the trials and tests. We go through the fire to get refined and purified. It helps when you change your perspective. It's all about your attitude towards it. Find the meaning. There is always something to learn – to gain.

I went through so much since saying "Yes" to God. I was living well in the world. I was having fun. Yet when I decided to follow Him, everything started coming at me, which confused me. I was doing the right things, yet bad was happening. But there is a reason and season for everything. Study the words of King Solomon in Proverbs and Ecclesiastes.

It's important to understand your season; Bad times don't last. There is a time for everything under the sun, as King Solomon said. But trust God through it all.

Endure because there is purpose through our pain. Our endurance builds our character and shows us what we are made of. Many times, we aren't aware of how strong we are until that is the only option we have.

You falling apart, of course, is an option, but where does that get you? You want to grow, right? Endure. This is a fight of faith—A good fight.

And as you go through, guess what you have to do? Praise Him! Yes! Praise should continually be in your mouth. (Hebrews 13:15) That shows trust in God, and it confuses the enemy. You will keep your eyes on God when you *actually* believe that He is and that He is the rewarder to those who diligently seek Him. I mean that deeply convicted *belief that brings about change in your life*. When you believe like that, you will praise Him in good times and bad.

Your face will be like a flint. Not looking to the right or left. This type of faith grows through endurance. I'm thankful for all the pain because I've gained spiritual maturation through it all and a closer relationship with God.

Today, with whatever you're going through, I want to encourage you to be still. (Psalm 46:10) Understand that nothing takes God by surprise, and nothing is too big for Him to handle.

God is a present help in times of trouble. Keep your eyes on Him during your storms while you're waiting, and you'll be walking on water! (Matthew 14:22-31)

YOUR WEEKLY CHALLENGE

This week ask yourself these reflection questions and look up the scriptures that are listed below. Read, pray, and meditate on what it says about endurance. Write down your answers.

Revelation 3:10-13 | James 1:2-4 | Philippians 4:13 | James 1: 12-17 | Isaiah 40:31 | Hebrews 10:26 | 2 Corinthians 4:16-18 |

What does it mean to endure hardships? What major difficulties have I endured and overcome since being saved?

Why does God allow trials to come upon me? How does this make me view God?

What attitude do I have while going through my trial? Do I have joy? Peace? Why or why not?

Why do I go through the same trials? What is God asking of me? Is anything changing?

How do I see myself: weak or strong? Why?

Do I believe that I am more than a conqueror? Why or why not? Do I understand times and seasons?

Saturday: How have I grown through my hardships? Was I surprised by anything that I learned about myself? If so, what?

PRAY

Lord God, I want to thank you for this day. Lord, you are my fortress, a present help in times of trouble. Help me to endure whatever trial comes upon me. Lord, go before this day and guide me everywhere you want me to go. It is not up to me to direct my steps. I thank you for your long-suffering. I thank you for your Spirit. Lord, I come to you to ask for an increase in my faith. Increase Lord. I need strength to endure. I look to you because you are where my help comes from. Lord, I ask for you to continue to cover my family and me. Open my spiritual eyes and ears so that I can hear what the Spirit is saying. I pray in the name of Jesus that the enemy does not deceive me. Help me to wait in expectation of your great works. Help me to seek your face in all that I do. You are my strength. Keep me, Lord. Keep me in perfect peace, and I promise to give you the praise, honor, and Glory that you deserve. In Jesus name, Amen

WEEK 4: DISCIPLINE

The ability to discipline yourself is paramount in your elevation

WEEKLY REFLECTIONS

During our walk with God, He is molding and teaching us His ways. The Bible has so many great nuggets to show us how to be wise in our everyday lives. God wants us to be honest, consult with other people, be humble, think before we speak, and have integrity, among other things.

We can't think that we don't play a role. We do. Yes, God will bless us and answer our prayers, but there are levels to this walk woman of God, and we have to play our part. Ephesians 5:15-20 gives us instructions. It says, *Be very careful, then, how you live—not as unwise but as wise, making the most of every opportunity, because the days are evil. Therefore, do not be foolish, but understand what the Lord's will is. Do not get drunk on wine, which leads to debauchery. Instead, be filled with the Spirit, speaking to one another with psalms, hymns, and songs from the Spirit. Sing and make music from your heart to the Lord, always giving thanks to God the Father for everything, in the name of our Lord Jesus Christ.*

Throughout the Bible, the Lord says what He requires of us. (1 Thessalonians 4:3| Proverbs 3:5-6)

We can't live any way we want, do as the world does, and treat God as a genie. We are asking Him to bless us with this or that but aren't willing to sacrifice daily. Jesus commissions us to take up our cross *daily*. (Luke 9:23) To go through to get through. It's a fight against our flesh. We must subdue it. It takes self-discipline. It won't "Just happen." I know many want it that way. I want it that way many times, so I get it. But the reality is that it won't.

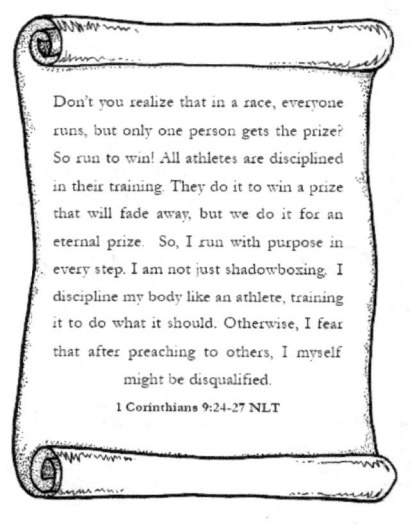

Don't you realize that in a race, everyone runs, but only one person gets the prize? So run to win! All athletes are disciplined in their training. They do it to win a prize that will fade away, but we do it for an eternal prize. So, I run with purpose in every step. I am not just shadowboxing. I discipline my body like an athlete, training it to do what it should. Otherwise, I fear that after preaching to others, I myself might be disqualified.
1 Corinthians 9:24-27 NLT

We all have a path set out for us by God, but we can go on a detour from that path by our decisions. We then blame God but not considering *our* ways. He is a Holy God! He requires holiness from us. (Jeremiah 29:11)

Stay close to God by staying in His Word and before Him in prayer. You can't know the things of God or what He wants for your life if you aren't spiritually connected to Him and His people. Abide in Him so that you can not only hear Him but know His will for your life.

Discipline is needed daily. It takes discipline and obedience. God is not partial, but there are levels, woman of God. Different experiences with God and the trials we endure bring forth a new way of thinking and a new revelation of who God is and who we are in Him. The more we go through with God, we grow, hence the more revelations we receive and the more levels we obtain. Level up!

I remember wanting God just miraculously to change things. I was like, "You are God, and You can do all things. Change it." But the Lord was asking me to do my part. Yes, He can do all things, but He will not force His will on us. We must pray and work in line with our prayers.

For example, you can't ask God to help you in your marriage if every time something goes wrong, you're packing your bags and ready to walk out the door. Or if the words you are speaking are contrary to building it up, they are tearing it down. That is not working in line *with* your prayer. Whatever your "thing," maybe. We all go through something, but it may not be the same thing at the same time. I know that we must show that we want this. We must take up our cross daily and follow God wherever that is. No, it isn't easy, but it's necessary.

We must make up our minds and put forth a strong effort to deny what our flesh wants to do. It will rise upon you as soon as you are trying to live for God. And it hurts. However, once you go through and endure, it gets better and easier each time, as your faith grows.

We have a choice. We can choose to do wrong or right. I know I make it sound simple, but truly that's because it is. It's like someone cutting you off on the road. You can choose to let it go or curse them out. We don't have to react to everything that comes our way. It takes daily practice, but it's doable if you make up your mind to do so. Finally, get the Word *in* you, and spend time in God's presence. If you want to see real results, you must make a real effort.

PRAY

Lord, I humbly approach your throne, thanking you for saving my life. Lord God, I thank you for the mercy you've shown me. I thank you for your love and saving grace. Lord, I want to know you on a deeper level. Guide me into all truth. Your Word is truth. Increase my wisdom Lord and give me a spirit of prayer. Lord, give me a yearning and desire for discipline to read your Word every day. Give me a spirit of discipline. No discipline seems pleasant at the time but painful. Later on, however, it produces a harvest of righteousness and peace for those trained by it. I want to be trained by it! I want the peace that comes from it! I want the structure and order that comes from following You. Forgive me of all the areas that I fall short. I also pray that I am not a stumbling block to anyone but that my light is shining, and they see you through my life. In Jesus' name. Amen.

YOUR WEEKLY CHALLENGE

This week ask yourself these reflection questions and look up the scriptures that are listed below. Read, pray, and meditate on what it says about discipline. Write down your answers.

Galatians 5:18-26 | 1 Timothy 4: 7-10 | James 3: 2-10 | 1 Peter 4: 7-16 | Hebrews 12:7 | Psalm 119: 9-11 | Hebrews 5: 11-14 |

Do I show discipline in my everyday life? How? Have I given up anything? What? And Why?

Why do I have to show discipline? How do I feel about that? What do I think about turning the other cheek? Do I practice this principle?

What does my lack of discipline say about me? Can I grow in my walk with a lack of discipline?

Have I made decisions that negatively affect my relationship with God? What about my natural and spiritual family? Friends? Co-workers?

What steps can I take this week to improve my self-discipline? At home? Work? And church?

Do I give up when it gets difficult? Why or why not?

Do I work in line with my prayers? Or do I pray one thing and do another?

SUMMARY OF WEEKS 1-4

So far, you've learned about grace, obedience, endurance, and discipline.

In the last month, what have you done differently?

Do you have a good understanding of God's grace? Do you understand and grasp the fact that He loves you with an everlasting love?

Do you understand what it means to be obedient? Have you started being obedient?

Do you grasp the concept of endurance? Do you understand how important it is for us to endure our trials? How endurance builds character? And that we as Saints are not immune to problems?

With that being the case, how important is having self-discipline? Compare your answer to your reality.

We can know things in theory, but until we put them into practice, it will be to no avail that we study.

It's the end of the week. Have you shown more self-discipline over the past week? Why or why not?

Write down what you've learned about yourself and God over the past four weeks?

WEEK 5: IDENTITY

You are a new creation in Christ, Live like it

WEEKLY REFLECTIONS

You are not required to change all at once, but you are required to change. Like the Israelites, you are on a journey toward the full possession of God's promises to you—and you will face trials and tribulations as you continue on this journey. But God has the same strategy for victory in your life as He had for His people centuries ago: little by little, from faith to faith.

> "This means that anyone who belongs to Christ has become a new person. The old life is gone; a new life has begun!"
>
> **2 Corinthians 5:17**

You will get where He wants you to go, one day and one victory at a time. Jesus said when He saves us, the old person is gone, so we must walk in that newness of life. It requires daily dying to self. It is a PROCESS. The word process is an action verb; it means a continuous action or series of changes in a definite matter.

Don't stop. Don't go backward. Move forward continually in what God has for you. He is already with you so you can do it. Whatever "it" is for you. Our *"its"* are different. But what's the same is this journey we are on with God. Again, don't stop! You are a new creation. Believe it and walk in that *today*.

Not the past; That's over. I don't live there, and neither do you. *Selah*

God is progressive, and He is moving forward. Move with Him. When you move into God's purposes for your life, the more effective you become for Him—and more of a threat you become to the kingdom of darkness.

BUT HOW CAN YOU MOVE IN YOUR PURPOSE IF YOU DON'T KNOW WHO YOU ARE?

My changes have come little by little, yet they are progressive. That's what you want to see—progression. You may not be where you want to be, but please, each day, make it your goal not to be where you were, even yesterday. Keep pushing forward.

You're NOT the same person. You mustn't beat yourself up when you make mistakes, yet equally important that you don't think it's ok to live as you were before being saved. It's a journey, yes, but there is a finish line. (Philippians 1:6) Keep moving forward. Press on! (Acts 20:24)

Walk with your head high! You're not defeated! The enemy doesn't want you to know who you are, so you walk defeated, depressed, and overwhelmed with the world. We are a Royal Priesthood. A holy nation. We must act like it. We must walk like it!

We must honor God with our lives! We are in the world, but we're not of this world. The more you learn about who you are in Christ, the more confidence you will have in your walk. God loves us! Set your mind on the things above. You came up from that water as a new creation; the old has passed away when you came up from that water.

Walk-in your newness woman of God! Walk-in authority as daughters of the Most High God! The great I Am! □□

This realization helped me to walk in confidence. I am God's child. People have been throwing the word "privilege" around—White privilege and Black privilege. Well, I am Black, but I claim KINGDOM PRIVILEGE. I am a child of God, and I identify that way above all others.

Hold your head up high, my sisters, because you are a daughter to the King of kings and Lord of lords.

PRAY

Heavenly Father, I thank you for your peace surpassing all thought and understanding peace that the world can't give. I thank you for constantly being a strong tower for me to run in. Thank you for making me new! Thank you for forgiving me. You said that I could come to you and find rest, and I thank you, God. I pray for peace in my home and work. I pray for strength to deal with the drama of the day and the craziness of the world. Go before me this day and set the crooked path straight, Lord. Allow me to be a blessing to someone today, Lord God. Help me to forgive those who have wronged me, Lord. I just want to walk in your peace. I want to walk in your ways and manifest the behavior as the new creation that I am. You have begun a good work in me, and I know that it won't end until your return. Continue to lead and guide me. My identity is in you. Show me, my purpose Lord. You said that you know the plans that you have for me. Guide me so that I am on the right path. Confirm my way. Lead me, Lord, throughout this day. In Jesus' name, Amen.

YOUR WEEKLY CHALLENGE

This week ask yourself these reflection questions and look up the scriptures that are listed below. Read, pray, and meditate on what it says about identity. Write down your answers.

1 John 3: 1-2 | John 15:16 | Hebrews 4:6 | Ephesians 1: 7-8 | Ephesians 2: 14-16 | Colossians 1:11 | Psalm 34:22 |

Am I doing the same thing I was doing before Jesus saved me? What's different?

Is my circle spiritual? Mixed? Has it changed?

Do I walk in the ways of the Spirit or the flesh? How do I know? What specifics can I pinpoint?

Do I trust in God's forgiveness? Am I holding on to past wrongs? Have I pardoned myself of past/present wrongs?

What am I entertaining? What do I watch and listen to? What types of conversations am I a part of? Do they honor God?

How do I identify myself? Do I get my validation from social media? How much time do I spend on social media? Do people know that I am a Christian? Do I live like a follower of Jesus?

What authority do I have as a child of God? Do I walk in my authority? Have I identified my purpose? If so, am I walking in it, and in what way? If not, what am I doing to discover my purpose?

WEEK 6: FAITH

Faith is a matter of belief and trust: not in what you see, but in what you don't

One of the things that stood out to me in this text was when it said: "Even when there was no reason to hope...." Sometimes we feel that way. That there is no reason to hope. That everything's been the same this long, why would it change now? Or even, "*How* will it change now?" You can be in a bad situation so long that you can't see your way out.

The challenge is believing in God *despite* what's happening around you—or how things have always been. Believing that God is who He says He is. And guess what? Simply saying, "I believe in God" is not even enough. That's basic; faith-filled action and obedience follow a true Believer in Jesus Christ. The Word says that even the demons believe, and they shudder. Belief goes along with faith, and faith without works is dead.

Knowing God exists and having a relationship with Him are two very different things. Our belief can be strong, lukewarm, or just about dead. How do you know where you are? The Word says we are to examine ourselves daily to see if we are in the faith. How do you do that? By daily evaluations. Check yourself with reflection questions. Reflect on your responses and behavior every day. Think on, and this may sound like a cliché', but "What would Jesus do?"

Having salvation is one thing. You are saved by grace, but don't stop there. That's just justification. There is more to this Christian walk. Faith without works is dead. It says so in the Word.

You must work your faith! Do you say you believe? Act like it. Speak your faith. Speak life! Speak the Word of God over yourself and your circumstances. Walk that thing out as Abraham did. He nev-

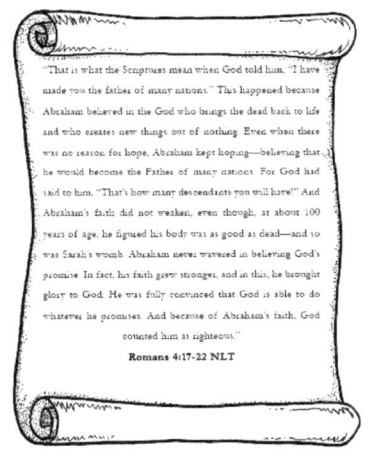

"That is what the Scriptures mean when God told him, 'I have made you the father of many nations.' This happened because Abraham believed in the God who brings the dead back to life and who creates new things out of nothing. Even when there was no reason for hope, Abraham kept hoping—believing that he would become the Father of many nations. For God had said to him, 'That's how many descendants you will have!' And Abraham's faith did not weaken, even though, at about 100 years of age, he figured his body was as good as dead—and so was Sarah's womb. Abraham never wavered in believing God's promise. In fact, his faith grew stronger, and in this, he brought glory to God. He was fully convinced that God is able to do whatever he promises. And because of Abraham's faith, God counted him as righteous."
Romans 4:17-22 NLT

er wavered in believing God's promises even though he and his wife were old. They didn't know how it would happen.

God only tells us things in part. But hold on to the part that He reveals. Remember and hold on to the words He gives you. In the Old Testament, they built altars to remember their encounters with God. What are your altars? What has He done for you that you can pinpoint?

What did God say about you? Whether you received it reading His Word, heard it from the pulpit, or received a Word from someone. Have Faith in Him. Trust Him. You can trust that. Not what you see. What you see is deceiving. God counts your faith as righteousness. We don't follow God for the benefits and blessings, but there are blessings and many benefits of following Him. It comes with the territory. Put Him first. Trust Him. Not just in Word but your deeds.

I remember thinking, how would I beat this cancer when people were dying every day from it? I didn't want it. I cried and asked the Lord if He could take it from me. My dad was dying from it! Things looked bad, but God said that I would live and not die, so I spoke that over my life regardless of its appearance. And it looked bad.

He also told me to "Be encouraged."

I had to keep speaking His Word. I looked up scriptures on healing and said them over myself daily.

I held on to His Word for my life! Literally!

PRAY

Father God, I thank you for this day. This is the day you have made, and I will rejoice and be glad in it. Lord God, I am overwhelmed by your goodness and mercy. I am so grateful that you've chosen me before the foundation of the world. Father, I pray that I continue to walk in your marvelous light. I pray for strength this day to walk in faith and not sight. I pray this day that I let my light shine wherever I go. Your Word is a lamp to my feet. I will shift the atmosphere when I enter a room. I am the righteousness of Christ. This day, Lord, I ask you to help me receive your love for me and help me to trust you more. Let me not lean on my understanding and, in all my ways, acknowledge you. I thank you and ask that you go before me this day and make the crooked path straight. Be with me throughout this week, Lord. I am seeking a deeper relationship with you, Lord. I want to know you intimately as my Father. Help me to decrease as you increase in my life. I pray for an increase Lord. Increase in faith. Increase in wisdom. Increase in discernment. More of you and less of me. I will walk in the authority that you have given me. I know that the enemy is a liar. I will trust you despite what it looks like because, Lord, I know you are well able. I thank you, Lord, and bless your name. In Jesus' name, Amen.

YOUR WEEKLY CHALLENGE

This week ask yourself these reflection questions and look up the scriptures that are listed below. Read, pray, and meditate on what it says about faith. Write down your answers.

Hebrews 11:6 | James 2:17 | Jeremiah 29:11 | Psalm 42:5 | Joshua 1:9 | Proverbs 3: 5-6 | 2 Corinthians 13:5

Am I trusting in what I see or what God has said? Do I have a living faith? Am I working it daily?

What has God told me about my situation? What have I said about my situation? What have I done with the Words I've received?

Do I believe Him? Am I confident that what He says is true? Why or why not? What am I basing it on?

Am I speaking the Word of God, or am I just reacting and responding to my situation and people? Am I proactive or reactive?

What are some ways that I can speak life into my circumstances? What am I willing to change going forward?

What do my actions say about my level of faith and trust? What about my words? In what areas can I increase my confidence in God?

What does He say that He will do when I trust Him? Why have I found it hard to trust God? Do I trust anyone? Why or why not?

WEEK 7: PRAYER

Communication is necessary for any successful relationship

WEEKLY REFLECTIONS

Prayer comes more easily when you're going through a trial. Even if that prayer is just, "Help!" Have you noticed that? When the storms are raging, you drop to your knees and cry out to God with no hesitation. But what about during the calm?

Prayer is a <u>necessity</u> in our Christian walk. It is how we communicate with God. To build on our relationship, we must talk to Him.

It's no different than building a friendship or being courted by a man. We talk. The Lord does talk back.

Prayer is also a way to let your request be made known. Let the Lord know what you need and want. Yes, He does know all things, but just like we want our children to come to us for help, the Lord wants us to come to Him for help. He wants to know that we depend on Him as our Father.

> Don't fret or worry. Instead of worrying, pray. Let petitions and praises shape your worries into prayers, letting God know your concerns. Before you know it, a sense of God's wholeness, everything coming together for good, will come and settle you down. It's wonderful what happens when Christ displaces worry at the center of your life.
>
> **Philippians 4: 6-7 MSG**

We also pray to intercede for others. It's important to lift people in prayer. Believe it or not, everyone can't get a prayer up. That's what the Word says. (Isaiah 1:15) (Proverbs 15:29) God calls us to be intercessors. Some people have a specific gift of Intercession, and they *really* go in. God lays people continually on their hearts. Yet as Believers, we are all called to lift our brothers and sisters up in prayer. (John 17: 18-21) (James 5:16)

How do you pray? Pray the Word of God. The Word has power, and the Word will do what it was sent to do and won't return to the Father void. He will perform His Word. Read it and gain an understanding of it so that when you're praying, you are effective.

We can't grow spiritually without a healthy prayer life. We must establish daily praying habits. It won't *just happen* either. This is something you have to be intentional in doing.

Regular and intentional praying started when I was recovering from my surgery: The Lord called me higher and told me to create a space for Him. I had an extra room in my house and set it aside to be my office/woman cave. How many know that didn't happen? That room is my prayer room. It's been anointed and set apart for God. He said He would meet me there, and He does. I pray when I wake. No particular time is set, just upon waking. And then a set time at noon and 8 pm daily. Regardless of where I am. Sometimes the prayer has to be silent. But I truly try to keep my appointments.

Suppose I can make sure to watch a television show at a particular time or a secular activity? In that case, I can be available for God in prayer. And He honors that.

It doesn't have to be lengthy to be powerful. It needs to be heartfelt, genuine, sincere, but most importantly, based on scripture.

The Word of God is our sword.

Too often, we are putting the Lord as an afterthought. We go on with our lives and remember Him when there is a problem. "Lord help me." "Save me." "Heal me." "Increase my finances." You get the idea. And there is nothing wrong with those prayers. Just make sure you have some, "Lord, I thank you…." "Lord, I love you…." "I ask you to bless so and so…" Make your request known, and also be thankful always. Ask for forgiveness in prayer. Repent of things you've done.

Never stop communicating with God. Be intentional about shutting out the outside noise so that you can hear Him.

PRAY

Lord, I just want to praise your name! I thank you, Lord Jesus, and I love you! Hallelujah! All things are new, and the old has passed away. Lord, my prayer for today is simply to say, "thank you." I give you all the Glory and the honor and the praise. You alone deserve it. You are faithful and true. There is none like you. You gave me the right to be your daughter! I am eternally grateful. You said you would never leave or forsake me, and I believe you, Lord, and I thank you. I love you. You rested on the 7th day, and today we can rest in you. I am so thankful for that. Keep my mind stayed on you, Lord God. I thank you for every lesson and blessing. I thank you for what you've already done, what you're doing, and what you're about to do. Thank you for the doors you're opening. God, I ask that you shut all the doors that you did not open. I'm thankful because you bless and add no sorrows. I ask that you strengthen me in my prayer life Lord. Give me a spirit of prayer. You say that I have not because I ask not. So, I'm asking Father. Purge me, Lord! Thank you for everything. In Jesus' name, Amen.

YOUR WEEKLY CHALLENGE

This week ask yourself these reflection questions and look up the scriptures that are listed below. Read, pray, and meditate on what it says about prayer. Write down your answers.

Colossians 4:2 | Jeremiah 29:12-14 | Psalm 145:18 | Hebrews 4:16 | James 4:2-3 | 2Chronicles 7:14 | Psalms 34:15

How often do I pray? How long do I pray? Am I distracted when I try to pray? Do I fight the distractions or give in?

Are my prayers mostly about me or others? Do I show gratitude to God in my prayers? Do I *know* God's Word? Do I pray according to God's Word?

Do I have forgiveness in my heart? Am I approaching the Lord while holding a grudge against someone?

How can I be sure God hears my prayer? Does He hear everyone's prayers? How do I know?

Do I feel closer to God? Has my faith increased? Write an example.

Do I pray with my husband? Children? Do I have any prayer partners? Why or Why not?

Have I been filled with God's Spirit? Do I pray in the Spirit? Do I believe in speaking/praying in tongues? Why or why not?

WEEK 8: FASTING

Deny yourself to FIND yourself

WEEKLY REFLECTIONS

Fasting is one of the hardest yet beneficial things we must do in our Christian walk. Many believers hear the Word "fasting," and they groan. They know the benefits, but the thought of denying oneself brings pain. Just the thought! However, intimidating a fast may be on the onset, its benefits far outweigh any negative connotation you can put with it.

Fasting and consecration go hand in hand. In general, fasting means to deny oneself food and drink or some variation of the two for an allotted time. Consecration is to deny yourself social media, television, and certain activities, to name a few. Consecration is time you choose to spend with God forsaking other things.

When you fast, it shows your body who is in charge. You also become keenly aware that you are weak. That you are flesh, and you need Jesus. Our flesh is very powerful, and as soon as we tell it, "No," it rises against us.

I know for a fact, from my own experiences and those around me, that we must fast to go higher in God. We need to bring our flesh into subjection and focus on our spirit. It takes self-discipline to fast, which we need to level up in our walk with God.

In our day-to-day life, we indulge and perhaps overindulge in whatever we want. The enemy loves that. When we deny ourselves and focus more on prayer and reading the Word, it matures us spiritually. We put ourselves in a position to hear God. To see and hear with our spiritual eyes and ears. Fasting humbles us. We know that we need God. We can't do anything apart from Him that is worth anything at all.

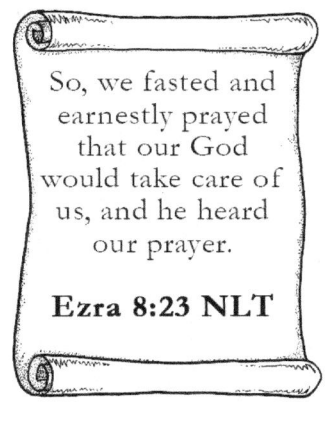

So, we fasted and earnestly prayed that our God would take care of us, and he heard our prayer.

Ezra 8:23 NLT

It's not unusual to start a fast and watch the clock. However, I want to offer some advice on fasting. *Don't watch the clock.* Fasting is a time of prayer, reading, and reflection. Don't focus on what you can't have. Instead, use the time wisely to focus on hearing what God is saying. When we quiet our flesh, our spirit gets louder. When we quiet our spirit, our flesh is more piercing. They are against one another and always will be.

When fasting, your flesh will act like its starving, but if you weren't on a fast and you just didn't eat for a few hours, there would be no problem. It's something about announcing it that you become accountable. There are countless mentions in the Bible of fasting and its wonderful benefits. Even Jesus fasted! Pray and ask God for strength.

Also, it must be a sacrifice! Sacrifices aren't easy. It must hurt—but press past the hurt. Don't focus on what you're giving up but on God. Read and pray.

Enter into the fast with a specific request from God because He honors our sacrifices. His answers are yes, no, and wait.

Check your motives for fasting as well. Make sure they are pure—don't think you are pulling a fast one on God. You're not.

You will find strength in a fast when you lean on the Lord. If you are truly in it, meditating on His Word and praying to Him, He will strengthen you. No one would know you were fasting unless you told them. He will sustain you during the fast.

When it's over, you become keenly aware that you are hungry for everything you denied yourself. If you fast long enough, you can break some bad habits. But you have to be willing to go through the pain that it will cause.

What are you willing to give up for God?

Make it a regular habit to fast, at the very minimum, once per week. Start today. You will be blessed by it.

PRAY

God, I thank you. I thank you for your reminders, your lessons, and your blessings. I thank you for your corrections. I thank you for reminding me daily of your love. This day, Lord, I ask you to help me receive your love for me and help me to trust you more. Help me to give up anything for you, Lord. I don't want to want anything more than you, Lord. Strengthen me and increase my faith. Help me to commit to a life of fasting. Give me a spirit of fasting, Jesus! I know that some powers of the enemy can't be broken except by fasting and prayer. I plead the blood of Jesus over my life and the life of my family. Help me to put you first in all things, knowing that you will supply all my needs. Check my motives, Lord. Bring to my mind anything that I need to repent of. Let me not lean on my understanding and, in all my ways, acknowledge you. I thank you and ask that you go before me this day and make the crooked path straight. Be with me throughout this week, Lord. I am seeking a deeper relationship with you, Lord. I want to know you intimately as my Father. Help me to decrease as you increase in my life. I pray for an increase Lord. Increase in faith. Increase in wisdom. Increase in discernment. More of you and less of me. I promise to give you the honor, glory, and all the praise in Jesus' name, Amen.

YOUR WEEKLY CHALLENGE

This week ask yourself these reflection questions and look up the scriptures that are listed below. Read, pray, and meditate on what it says about fasting. Write down your answers.

Acts 3:19 | Matthew 4:2 | Acts 13:3 | Matthew 6: 16-18 | Luke 2:37 | Deuteronomy 9:9 | Zechariah 7:5 |

Am I willing to fast? How often? What day will I fast? What am I willing to give up?

What does it mean to sacrifice? Who have I sacrificed for? In what ways have I sacrificed for God?

Do I stop fasting when it hurts? Can I endure? Am I willing to go through the pain for the Glory?

What examples can I pinpoint to show that I am willing to sacrifice for God? Do I have things that I want to change? Behaviors or patterns I need to break?

(After Fast) after fasting, what have I learned about myself this week?

(After Fast) Did I seek God's face regularly during my fasting? Did I hear His voice?

(After Fast) Have I discovered the benefits of fasting and prayer? What were they?

SUMMARY OF WEEKS 5-8

This month you've learned about identity, faith, prayer, and fasting. What did you realize that you didn't know before regarding these topics?

Have you started anything new this month regarding prayer and fasting? What has been the outcome?

Did you create a daily prayer schedule? Write it here:

In what ways did you fast? How did you quiet the noise to hear God more? Did you slowdown from social media this month? Television watching?

Write down your thoughts for these past four weeks related to the topics of identity, faith, prayer, and fasting.

Did you go into fasting with a request? Was it answered?

What have you learned about yourself and God over the past four weeks?

WEEK 9: DOUBLE-MINDEDNESS

Sometimes you don't know you can do it until you actually do it. So, DO it

WEEKLY REFLECTIONS

What an amazing scripture! It's very plain, isn't it? Straight to the point. Elijah said choose, and they were silent. People ride the fence because they think it's safe. People don't answer questions because they want to remain neutral. They stay out of situations where they are forced to decide "for" or "against." In bible study, when the Pastor asks a question, many speak amongst themselves or quietly to the one sitting next to them but do not raise their hands. I've done it myself. I'm sure one of the reasons is fear of getting it wrong. Being quiet is safe.

Do you fear getting it wrong in your walk with God? Do you straddle the fence because you are playing it safe?

Elijah asked the Israelites what they were going to do. He was telling them that it's fine either way. But they needed to decide. He asked them to choose this day whom they will serve: Jehovah or Baal. I pose that question to you: Who do you prefer? Jesus or Satan?

You will say one name out of your mouth but pay attention to what your behavior says. Satan could care less what you say out of your mouth or how often you go to church. Instead, He cares about the sanctification of your life. Now that's a true witness to the power of God.

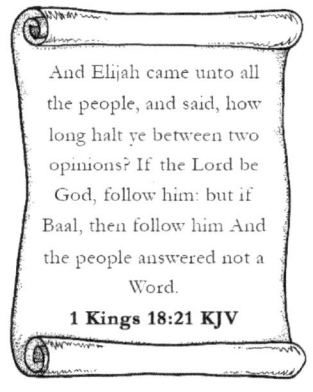

And Elijah came unto all the people, and said, how long halt ye between two opinions? If the Lord be God, follow him: but if Baal, then follow him And the people answered not a Word.
1 Kings 18:21 KJV

When Elijah posed that question, they stood quiet because they were of two minds. They wanted to go back and forth, not fully committing to either lifestyle. You may be the woman who parties and drinks and hangs around many secular people or professed Christians but not living a life Holy unto God. That is a double-minded person. That is what Elijah was asking in the scripture.

I can speak on that because I was a double-minded Christian at one point, yet I didn't know it. God revealed that to me. I believed the lie that I could do whatever I wanted because God knew my heart. He sure did! Do you tell yourself that?

You may have one foot in the church and one in the world. You're lukewarm, and your heart is far removed. You see, you know where you are more than anyone except God. You can change it too. If you expect to go higher, you cannot be double-minded. Period. There is no negotiation here. You must make up your mind, who is God? Follow Him.

STRONGHOLDS ARE REAL!

DEMONS ARE REAL!

Many people have strongholds of one thing or another. It is a faulty thinking pattern based on lies and deception

(2 Corinthians 10:5 KJV Casting down imaginations, and every high thing that exalteth itself against the knowledge of God, and bringing into captivity every thought to the obedience of Christ ;)

Cast them down! You can do it, especially if you have the Holy Spirit inside you. But even if you don't have the Holy Spirit yet, you can cast those thoughts down that exalts itself against the knowledge of God. This is something you should work on daily.

The enemy hasn't changed in his tactics. The same lie he told Eve is the same one he uses today, "Did God really say?"

(Genesis 3:1 NLT. The serpent was the shrewdest of all the wild animals the Lord God had made. One day he asked the woman, "Did God really say you must not eat the fruit from any of the trees in the garden?")

What he does is implant doubt in your mind. He makes you second guess God, among other things. He especially comes after us, the believer. We must be watchful because the Word says that the devil walks around like a roaring lion seeking whom he can devour. But the good thing is that it also says that if we submit to God and resist the devil, he will flee.

PRAY

Lord God of grace, I thank you for this day. Father, I humbly approach your throne, asking for mercy. I repent for any area that I displayed double mindedness. You said that a double-minded man is unstable in all his ways. Lord, help me in any area that I am unbalanced. Help me to be stable! Have mercy on me, Jesus! I believe in you, and I know that you are the only living God. The true God. I thank you for saving my life and showing me grace and mercy. Forgive me and strengthen me as I continue in boldness in my journey. I want to be an example and not a stumbling block to anyone. Continue to help me grow in my walk with you, Lord. I bind the plans of the enemy. I decree and declare new beginnings and a new season in my life right now, Lord! The devil is bound and crushed. He is under my feet! Forgive me for not being mindful and taking heed to Your Word. I will go forth with a sound mind in victory! Send a fresh anointing Lord! I thank you, and I love you. In Jesus' name. Amen.

YOUR WEEKLY CHALLENGE

This week ask yourself these reflection questions and look up the scriptures that are listed below. Read, pray, and meditate on what it says about being double-minded. Write down your answers.

James 1:8 | James 4:8 | Isaiah 29:13 | Matthew 6:24 | James 4:4 | Revelation 3:15-18 | 1 Corinthians 10:21 |

What does it mean to be lukewarm? Am I double-minded? How can playing it safe harm me?

How have I been living my life? What does the Bible say about being unstable? Does my social media persona reflect my true self?

If I trust God, then why is it hard for me to make decisions? Do I have one foot in the world and one in the church? Is my devotion divided?

Who is Baal? Do I serve him? How do I know? What do my actions say?

Who is Jesus? Do I serve Him? How do I know? What do my actions say?

Do I take a stand for God when given the opportunity? Am I afraid of what others will say? What do my actions say?

In what ways will I make up my mind? What changes am I willing to make going forward?

WEEK 10: RENEWAL

Change your thinking: Understanding comes as you continue to seek the deeper things of God

WEEKLY REFLECTIONS

I love how this version puts this scripture. Also, compare with the amplified version of the Bible. It is plain. There can be no mistakes as to the meaning of it. Our minds are powerful. We can think of ourselves as healed or sick in many cases.

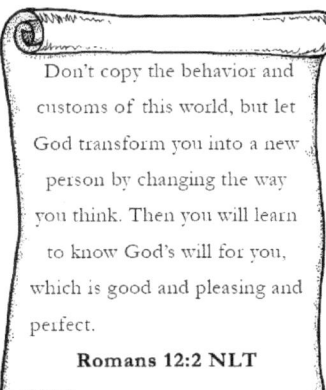

Don't copy the behavior and customs of this world, but let God transform you into a new person by changing the way you think. Then you will learn to know God's will for you, which is good and pleasing and perfect.

Romans 12:2 NLT

We can cause ourselves to believe in things that aren't there and tell ourselves that we are amazing until we start to believe it. Have you heard the term, "You are what you say you are?" Well, words were first thoughts. Your thoughts turn into actions. If you are focusing on Godly principles, your actions will reflect that. If you are focusing on self or the world, your actions will likewise reflect that.

Having a renewed mind is paramount in going higher in your walk with God. You can't think the same. The Word says to have the mind of Christ. (Philippians 4:7) This, my sister, is a daily concept.

The idea is to check yourself and your thoughts every day. Don't just react to what comes your way. We have a real part to play in this walk, and the battleground is in mind.

Again, you must be intentional. There's that word again. But it's true.

When we turn on our televisions and open up our social media apps, we are inundated with all types of propaganda contrary to our Christian beliefs. We entertain some of it. But you better know when to shut it down. You have to be mindful that too much time is spent in worldly affairs.

You will know because your conversation and behavior will change. There is a lot of violence and racial things going on. We have to be careful with all of it. We are the first children of God. Don't lose sight of that and get caught up in what's going on in the world. Your renewed mind says that Jesus is returning. Your renewed mind recalls scripture that says we are in the last days and lawlessness shall increase. It tells how the days will be like Noah's. With those things in mind, you keep a proper perspective on world affairs. As Christians, we pray. We pray for our country, leaders, and citizens.

The enemy also comes to us, putting thoughts in our minds. He sets up strongholds. A stronghold can come in the way of addiction, pride, lack of faith, doubt, lack of forgiveness, etc.

We must be aware that it is a very real threat. We are not immune, but we can cast those thoughts down. We fight with our spiritual armor. (Ephesians 6: 14-17) We have to withstand and fight the enemy using the Word of God. You can't resist him if you don't know your Word. Reading and meditating on your Word will help you to grow in maturity.

You will know you are growing when your responses change from your flesh to your spirit. You won't have to be out here struggling, looking for your purpose if you are in the will of God. He will reveal it to you and progressively transform you in this journey. But don't fight the process. Yield to God and what He is trying to do in you. He's trying to change you.

Your thoughts will start to line up with scripture. That is a sign of maturity. Things that you once thought were ok will change. I used to live a life as a bisexual woman. I felt that life was ok at one time. I used to be a heavy drinker and marijuana smoker. I used to have a short temper and was quick to fight. And many other ways that were changed, but it started with a change in my thinking. And it has happened over the years from faith to faith with different situations. Slowly my mind was being renewed.

As I started to get closer to God, I realized that it wasn't the life that He wanted for me. It was a trap. A trap that started from molestation as a child. You see, our minds are all screwed up from so many things— Many of which we carry from childhood. Our minds aren't renewed right away after baptism. We are new people when we come out of the water, but we don't believe it right away because nothing changed yet. It takes time. God does strive with us. He knows us, and as long as we work towards being a better us, He is there.

Our minds change from what we once thought was acceptable behavior to what God says is acceptable. Not social media. Not society, family, or friends, but what God says, even down to how we dress. We change and become more modest as we grow in Christ. We are all on different levels of growth. That is why it's important not to be a stumbling block to anyone.

Be an example woman of God. Renew your mind. There is peace when you do that. You won't fall all out when things are falling apart around you. I know this firsthand. God is faithful. He's given me the peace that surpasses all understanding, and you can have that too.

PRAY

Lord, I need you today. You are a mind regulator, and I am asking for a renewed mind. I am thankful for your saving grace, and I realize that I play a part in my walk with you. I have to take up my cross daily and follow you. Lord, I thank you because you care about me. You care enough about me to send me reminders and to bless me even when I don't have it all together. I want to go higher in a relationship with you, Lord. I will set my mind on things above and not on this earth. Today, I say "Yes!" I want to live a life fully sold out to you. Hear my heart today, Lord. Strengthen me. I want my mind to stay on those things that are pleasant and uplifting. I want to speak life into people and situations. Your Word is truth. I cast down any thought that exalts itself against the knowledge of you and brings into captivity every thought to the obedience of Christ. I thank you this day for your love and mercy. In Jesus' name, Amen.

YOUR WEEKLY CHALLENGE

This week ask yourself these reflection questions and look up the scriptures that are listed below. Read, pray, and meditate on what it says about renewing your mind. Write down your answers.

Philippians 4:8 | Ephesians 4:22-32 | 2 Corinthians 10:3-6 | Colossians 3: 2-10 | Romans 7:25-26 | Romans 8:6-8 | Romans 7:14-25

What are my thinking patterns? Have they changed since being saved? Am I nicer to people? Do I turn the other cheek or seek revenge?

What influences my thoughts? The Bible? The world? Do I think like the world or God? How do I know?

(If married) How do I view my role as a wife? Do I respect my husband? Am I a helpmeet? Do I show love?

How can I daily work on my thoughts? What can I do today to line my thoughts up with what God says?

Can someone look at my life and see God? Do I post on social media? Am I honest? Do I talk about my faith?

Do I think positive thoughts? How do I handle my negative thoughts and emotions? How involved am I in the political and social climate?

Am I aware of any strongholds? How can I cast them down? Am I overwhelmed? How can I have peace of mind?

WEEK 11: SIN

Sin is deceptive. Don't be fooled

WEEKLY REFLECTIONS

Romans 6:15 is such an amazing scripture. It truly gets to the heart of the matter. Many Christians are looking for loopholes. Yes, it's true. I know of some. In fact, I was one of those at one point in my life. Saying things like, "Weed is an herb, and God says the herbs were all good." These are lies we tell ourselves and the deceptiveness of sin.

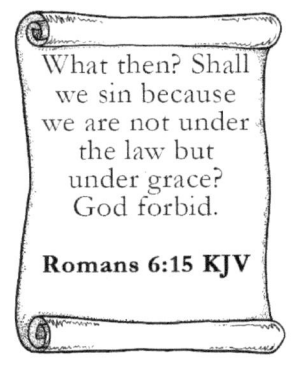

What then? Shall we sin because we are not under the law but under grace? God forbid.

Romans 6:15 KJV

Sin is bondage. Plain and simple. You can't dance with the devil and come out unscathed. There is no freedom in sin, only in God. You become a slave to sin as your master.

In the world, I had the mindset that I could do whatever I wanted. Consequences? What consequences? I was living life and dared anyone to say anything. Once I became saved, that mindset didn't change right away. After being rescued from the world, I walked the right path until hard times would come, and I would go back to my vices. I know that your mind has to change for your actions to change. God does not, nor can He, operate in sin. He is Holy and calls us to holiness.

The Bible speaks of sin in the King James Version 749 times! He wants to warn us. Jesus paid a heavy price, and we must understand that our Lord Jesus Christ died for us. Why would we live a life contrary to what He wants for us?

Sin can look enticing. In fact, it *is* enticing. Many times, we look at people not following God, and they are prosperous. They may not have similar problems. But I want you to know that your worst day with God is better than your best day without Him. Don't be deceived; social media glorifies sin, and nothing is off-limits. Do whatever you want is the way of the world.

Don't sin. Do I make it sound simple? I know it isn't. But I want you to be mindful and purposeful in this walk, woman of God. Trusting God will help you not to sin. Trust Him, so you don't fall into the traps of sin. Trust Him to provide for you, so you don't steal. Please don't love money so much that you do dumb stuff to get it. Trust God with your livelihood.

There are traps out there. We must tread carefully. It's a progressive thing. I am speaking as a person who was lukewarm to now being on fire for Jesus! Having a made-up mind and completely sold out. I want that for you as well.

We have the freedom to do what we like. The Bible says there is no condemnation for us, yet everything is not profitable for us. Everything is not good for us to do. God wants to protect us. He loves us.

We think we are in control when dabbling in sin. We aren't. The wages of sin is death. That's the Word. Take it seriously. Submit yourself to God. Resist the devil, and he will flee.

What is sin? Do you know how the Word of God defines it? The Bible describes sin as a transgression of the law of God and rebellion against God. Independence of God and plainly, falling short or missing the mark. Who doesn't miss the mark? (1 John 3:4) (Deuteronomy 9:7) We've inherited sin through Adam. Read the story of his rebellion in Genesis 3.

We need Jesus and the covering that His shed blood provides us. Sin separates us from God. Jesus reconciles us.

Although there are degrees of sin, every sin, every act of rebellion, leads to condemnation and eternal death (Romans 6:23)

We can't make a practice of sinning. (1 John 3:9) A practice means something we are doing over and over. When we recognize the sin, we must repent and turnaround from it. We have the power through the Holy Spirit to do so.

You will have times where you fail God. Pray and ask for God to forgive you. He has grace for you.

We say that we aren't to judge one another, but in the body of Christ, what does the Word say? Read 1 Corinthians 5.

Get in the habit of reading the Word so that you know what it says for yourself. Don't justify your sin. Acknowledge it. Repent and move on. Don't be the Christian woman who says, "Don't judge me because my sin is different than yours." More on that in part 2.

We do reap what we sow. I know I have. We speak of the blessings of God, but He also chastens and corrects us. But that's love. He loves us. (Proverbs 3:12)

PRAY

Father God, I thank you for your grace and mercy. Thanking you for making me your daughter. I thank you for another day of life. Another change to get it right. You say your mercies are rare new every day, and I thank you for that. I come to you today and ask you for forgiveness. Forgive me for any sin that I've committed against you. I want to walk in holiness and sanctification. Help me, Father! I am your daughter, and I want to represent you as such. I want my life to bring you, Glory. Create in me a clean heart and renew a right spirit within me. I belong to you, and the enemy can't have me. No weapon formed against me shall prosper! I thank you for teaching and guiding me in my walk. I thank you for taking me from faith to faith. I trust you; I love you, and I give you all the honor, praise, and Glory that's due you. In Jesus' name, Amen.

YOUR WEEKLY CHALLENGE

This week ask yourself these reflection questions and look up the scriptures that are listed below. Read, pray, and meditate on what it says about sin. Write down your answers.

1 John 1:9-10 | 1 Corinthians 6: 9-10 | 1 John 1:6-10 | Romans 3:19-24 | Proverbs 14:12 | 1 Samuel 12:20 | Romans 6:14

What is the Bible's definition of sin? Do I sin? Does my life glorify God?

How have I viewed sin before being saved? How do I view it now? Is my conscience clear? What is my attitude towards sin?

Do I think my sin is greater or lesser than someone else? What does the Bible say?

Do all sins lead to death? Do I believe in Heaven and Hell? Why or why not?

Why do I sin? When do I sin the most? Do I have sin partners? [Enablers] What changes am I prepared to make?

What have I discovered about myself that I didn't know before? Do I seek after friendships with people living as I do? Am I trying to elevate in my walk?

Am I honest with myself and my walk with God? Do I understand that I have to work out my salvation?

WEEK 12: FREEDOM

We are not bound, except the boundaries we put on ourselves

WEEKLY REFLECTIONS

We are truly free. Truly. We are free to live a life of willful sin or to live a life free of sin. Realization and appreciation are what make a difference—having the understanding that nothing can keep you bound because of Jesus' death on the cross. He died so that you and I can have life. Nothing can keep us bound except what we put on ourselves, even when the enemy comes with his temptations. We can rebuke that and cast those thoughts down, and keep it moving. It's a daily process, but it's worth it. Once you realize who you are in God, it should give you boldness to walk in the freedom that Jesus gives.

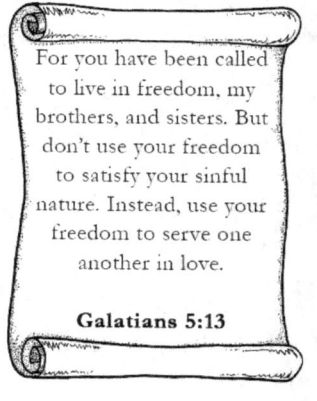

For you have been called to live in freedom, my brothers, and sisters. But don't use your freedom to satisfy your sinful nature. Instead, use your freedom to serve one another in love.

Galatians 5:13

So, we realize the truth of freedom, but we must also appreciate it. We must fill our minds with the Word and receive the love of Jesus. We don't have to succumb to the deceitfulness of the world.

We see it for what it is. The veil has been removed. Your new mind brings new attitudes, emotions, and practices. You are free to live a sanctified life! This leads to right living and holiness.

You begin to live this set apart life as a "peculiar" person unto God. (1 Peter 1:2-9) Not because you "have" to, but because you appreciate what was done for you, and you do it out of love. Why wouldn't you want to live the way the Bible says to live? Love God with all your heart and your neighbor. If people just did this, the world would be an amazing place. Free from all the terrible woes we face today. Love covers a multitude of sins.

True freedom brings joy. You understand that no outside stimuli are responsible for your joy, happiness, and peace and that it is all connected to your heavenly Father.

As I've mentioned many times, my life changed for the better. I became free in my mind going through this cancer journey. I say, "In my mind" because I was already free, but I wasn't living like it. I knew in theory that I was free. I read it. I heard the Pastors preaching it, but I didn't feel free.

Are you living like you are free or bound? Jesus set you free, my sister. Whom the Son sets free is free indeed. (John 8:36)

We have everything we need. We are fully equipped, right now, today. But the difference is coming to an understanding and walking and resting in it. Your actions will change. Your thoughts and words will change.

There's a quote by Tony Robbins that says, "Remember, a real decision is measured by the fact that you've taken a new action. If there's no action, you haven't truly decided."

I thought that was deep and appropriate. So, what now? Have you taken new action? You are free.

PRAY

Lord God of Grace, I thank you for your grace and mercy. I thank you for being who you are. My Savior. My prince of peace. My Lord. I thank you for going to the cross for me. I thank you for your courage and your love. I thank you for bearing my sins so that I can live and be free! I ask today that you continue to strengthen me and go before me. This day, this week, this month, Lord! Bring to my remembrance all the scriptures I've read and the lessons I've learned. Let me walk in your ways. In the newness of life. Keep your Word in my mind and heart. Your Word is truth. Please keep my mind in perfect peace as I keep it stayed on you. Let me walk in the freedom that you gave me. I will not walk in sin. Nothing will have me in bondage again. My life belongs to you, and no weapon formed against me shall prosper! Keep me under the shelter of your wings, Lord. I thank you for your covering and protection, Lord. I thank you for a new mind. I give you all the honor, praise, and Glory that's due to you. In Jesus' name, Amen.

YOUR WEEKLY CHALLENGE

This week ask yourself these reflection questions and look up the scriptures that are listed below. Read, pray, and meditate on what it says about your freedom in Christ. Write down your answers.

2 Corinthians 3:17-18| Galatians 5:1| Romans 6:22-23| John 8:32| Isaiah 61:1-3| John 17:14-17| 1John 2:15-17

What is the definition of freedom? Is there a difference between the world's definition and the Bible?

Do others control my behavior? What does freedom in Christ mean to me? Do I live free?

Does someone have the power based on their words or actions to alter my behavior? My day?

Do I make moves based on what someone else says? What is truth?

Am I living the way I want? Am I happy? Why? Why not? Am I just existing? Or living?

What did Jesus' death on the cross mean for me?

What does "being in the world but not a part of the world" mean to me? Can I still have fun living saved?

SUMMARY OF WEEKS 9-12

Over the past 12 weeks, you've been studying grace, obedience, endurance, self-discipline, identity, faith, prayer, fasting, and stability of the mind, the renewal of your mind, sin, and freedom.

What's next? Reflection is always best. Suppose you have an accountability partner that works great as well. Have you started anything new this month regarding having a double mind, renewing your mind, and walking in freedom from sin?

What did you learn that you didn't know before regarding these topics? What has been the outcome?

Do you feel closer to God? Has your faith increased so far?

What have you learned about yourself and God over the past four weeks?

WORD-BASED AFFIRMATIONS

- I AM THE HEAD AND NOT THE TAIL.
- I AM A LENDER AND NOT A BORROWER.
- BY HIS STRIPES, I AM HEALED.
- I AM THE RIGHTEOUSNESS OF CHRIST.
- GOD WILL PERFECT THAT WHICH CONCERNS ME.
- ALL THINGS WILL WORK FOR THE GOOD OF THOSE WHO LOVE GOD AND ARE CALLED TO HIS PURPOSE.
- I AM CALLED ACCORDING TO HIS PURPOSE, AND THINGS WILL WORK OUT FOR ME.
- GOD IS NOT A MAN THAT HE SHOULD LIE.
- WHAT HE SAYS WILL COME TO PASS.
- GOD SAYS HIS WORD WILL NOT RETURN TO HIM VOID.
- IT WILL DO WHAT HE PURPOSES FOR IT TO DO.
- GOD WILL NEVER LEAVE OR FORSAKE ME.
- GOD KNEW ME BEFORE THE FOUNDATION OF THE WORLD.
- GOD IS MY PROVIDER.
- IN ALL MY WAYS, I WILL ACKNOWLEDGE HIM, AND HE WILL SET MY PATH STRAIGHT.
- NOTHING IS TAKING GOD BY SURPRISE. HE KNOWS ALL THINGS.
- I CAN TRUST THE LORD IN MY SITUATION.
- I AM GOD'S MASTERPIECE
- I AM A NEW CREATURE IN CHRIST
- I AM A SPIRIT BEING ALIVE TO GOD
- I AM A BELIEVER, AND THE LIGHT OF THE GOSPEL SHINES IN MY MIND
- I AM A DOER OF THE WORD AND BLESSED IN MY ACTIONS
- I AM A JOINT-HEIR WITH CHRIST
- I AM MORE THAN A CONQUEROR THROUGH HIM WHO LOVES ME
- I AM AN OVERCOMER BY THE BLOOD OF THE LAMB AND THE WORD OF MY TESTIMONY
- I AM A PARTAKER OF HIS DIVINE NATURE
- I AM AN AMBASSADOR FOR CHRIST

REFERENCES

https://www.2knowmyself.com/how_childhood_experiences_affect_adulthood

https://psychcentral.com/blog/archives/2016/03/12/how-childhood-trauma-affects-adult-relationships/

https://www.viralbeliever.com/bible-studies/transparent-christian/

Carm.org

www.gotquestions.org

https://www.biblegateway.com/

Jollynotes.com

https://www.joycemeyer.org/everydayanswers/ea-teachings/knowing-who-i-am-in-christ

AFTERWARD

This book was a labor of love, from my heart to yours. I thank God for putting this on my heart to do. I remember waking up from a dream and this book being downloaded to me. I knew the layout and everything immediately. I went to my computer and started typing at 7 am and typed all day until the evening. That was my first rough draft. Prior, I had another devotional I was working on, yet He said that was for a later date.

I am in awe of my Heavenly Father. He took me to higher levels during my cancer journey and the mourning of both my parents. *(I still mourn their loss)*

For this book, He pressed upon me the importance of not only being on one accord and uplifting one to another, but we need to elevate in our walk with Him. We will be effective in our disciple-making if we are living it and not just talking about it. People watch what we do more than what we say.

Thanks for your support and continue to show the love of Christ. I pray that you were able to get something positive out of this book.

Do you want to publish a book? Contact me at:

www.tuckerpublishinghouse.com

If you've enjoyed this book, please leave a brief review at the online bookseller of your choice. Many thanks for considering my request.

Tag me @iamtaratucker on Instagram for any videos, excerpts, or book clubs with the hashtag #Iamgoinghigher

ACKNOWLEDGEMENTS

I want to give thanks to the Lord for not only saving my life but engrafting me into the beautiful body of Christ. Thank you, Lord, for your revelations and the amazing peace you have given me that defies all logic and understanding.

RIP to my mom and dad: You are forever loved and missed.

I thank my husband, Frank, for his love and commitment to me. I love you.

I thank my children, Tyler, Devin, and Deonta' for their love and support. You are the sun that shines after the rain.

I thank the JEWELS, Ladies of Prayer. Let's continue to put the Lord first and encourage each other daily.

I thank my Lam Church family! You are amazing! Thank you for all your prayers and support through it all! I can't name you all, but I love and appreciate you.

I thank my natural family for loving me and supporting me through my journey.

And thank you to all of you who have continued to support me throughout the years. Blessings to you!

ABOUT THE AUTHOR

Tara Tucker is a Visionary, Publisher, Speaker, Certified Life, and Solution-Focused Coach, and Author of several books, including her bestseller, Everybody Kneeling ain't Praying. Tara is also a Book Writing Consultant, helping Kingdom-Driven Women own their stories and complete their books with clarity and confidence. She owns Tucker Publishing House, LLC, Founder and President of the nonprofit Jewels LOP Outreach and an Elite Women Organization Board member. She also founded Beni Publishing, an offshoot from her main company creating a space for children to use their creativity and share their voices. Tara is the Host of Going Higher Together and cohost of Her Story Podcast. Tara's heart is for the people of God to walk in their freedom, to live, love, and BE authentic.